A MACDONALD BOOK

Text copyright © 1988 Denny Robson
Illustrations copyright © 1988 David West

First published in Great Britain in 1988
by Macdonald & Co (Publishers) Ltd
London & Sydney
A member of Maxwell Pergamon Publishing Corporation plc

Photoset in 16pt Rockwell by Keene Graphics Ltd, London
Colour origination by Scantrans Pte Ltd, Singapore

Printed and bound in Spain
by Cronion SA

Macdonald & Co (Publishers) Ltd
Greater London House
Hampstead Road
London NW1 7QX

BRITISH LIBRARY CATALOGUING IN PUBLICATION DATA
Robson, Denny
Fred, Frederick and Captain Hook.
I. Title II. West, David
823'.914[J]

ISBN 0-356-16449-7
ISBN 0-356-16450-0 Pbk

Denny Robson

Fred Frederick
AND CAPTAIN HOOK

Illustrated by David West

Macdonald

For
Jonny, Alex and Jamie

Chapter One

The alarm rang. Fred thrashed around his bed wrestling with his teddy. His eyes were tight shut and he growled occasionally. Fred was dreaming.

Fred spent most of his time dreaming. Even during the day.

He loved to dream he was someone else. Someone who was brilliant at everything and who never got into trouble. Not ordinary old Fred, but the superhero Frederick!

This morning he was dreaming he was Frederick, fighting a savage bear. A crowd of onlookers cheered – and then a strange thing happened. The bear spoke.

"Get a move on Fred," it growled, sounding a bit like his dad.

The heroic Frederick was puzzled.

"GET UP FRED!" it roared in his dad's voice.

Fred opened his eyes and saw his dad leaning over his bed.

"I said get up Fred. It's time for school." Dad took a beaten-up teddy out of Fred's bed and pulled its arms back into place.

"Today's not just any old day, you know," he said. "Remember? Here's a clue."

To Fred's surprise he started hopping round the room, muttering about dead men's chests.

"He's gone mad," Fred thought with a yawn.

Then he remembered. It was the play this afternoon! His class was performing an exciting bit from *Peter Pan*. And he was going to be the pirate Captain Hook.

Fred leapt out of bed and started to pull on his clothes.

Trust Dad to get it wrong.

"Hook's got one arm, not one leg," he shouted as his dad hopped out of the room.

Captain Hook! Fred didn't think he was very good at acting.

In fact, Fred thought he wasn't much good at most things.

So he'd been surprised when Mrs Scott had chosen him. She'd probably forgotten her glasses that morning. (Mrs Scott was called 'The Bat' because she couldn't see a thing without her glasses and she flapped a lot.)

Fred finished getting dressed, feeling worried. He was sure his mind would go blank during the play. He'd been trying all week, but he still kept forgetting his lines.

"Don't worry," said his mother at breakfast time. "It won't be that bad. Just pretend you're a pirate."

"It's not that simple," said Fred glumly, looking at himself in the mirror. Small, round and shiny, with glasses to match. Hardly the scourge of the seven seas!

"But if I were a pirate," he thought, drifting off into a daydream – he was Frederick the Fearsome on the high seas with skull and crossbones – "I'd make Alice Green walk the plank. Straight away."

Alice was one of Fred's classmates. She had wanted to be Captain Hook. She had to play one of his pirates instead, and she seemed to think it was all Fred's fault.

Imagining Alice Green fleeing from a crocodile, Fred sugared his toast and spooned marmalade into his tea. And he didn't even notice the funny taste.

Chapter Two

At school that morning nothing seemed to go right. Mrs Scott had turned into a dragon and Fred was thinking about the play so much he couldn't concentrate.

"You're hopeless," sniggered Alice Green when Fred got told off for the fifth time for dreaming.

"And you'll be just the same this afternoon. They should have picked me."

Fred wished they had. In fact he wished they'd picked her, frozen her and packaged her. Like a frozen bean.

"Alice Green, the frozen bean, the silliest pirate you've ever seen," Fred hummed, and got told off for the sixth time.

15

"What's the matter, Fred?" asked Tom Dent at break-time. Tom was Fred's best friend.

"It's the play," said Fred gloomily. "I'm sure I'm going to forget my lines!"

"No problem!" said Tom brightly. "We'll practise your lines together at lunch-time."

Fred smiled for the first time that day. Tom was good at remembering lines. He was going to be Peter Pan. He would sort things out.

After break, Fred tried to pay attention. But it didn't last long. Mrs Scott began telling the class about the first men on the moon.

"As they stepped on to the moon's surface," she said, sliding her glasses up and down her nose in a way Fred liked to copy, "the captain said, 'that's one small step for a man, but a giant leap for mankind'."

Fred forgot all about paying attention and he began to daydream again. He could imagine a different scene altogether . . .

The captain is about to plant the flag when he looks round and sees ... Frederick Flyby, world's greatest astronaut. Frederick has beaten them to it!

"Thought you were never going to get here," says Frederick to the astonished captain. "Nothing much here, mind. Rocks, lots of dust, the occasional two-headed alien ..."

The captain shakes Frederick's hand and says ...

"STOP SLOUCHING FRED!"

Mrs Scott pulled Fred up in his chair.

"Now sit up straight," she said, peering at him through her thick glasses. "And tell the class everything I've been saying."

Alice Green snorted behind her hanky.

Fred couldn't remember.

"Well," he began, "landing on the moon was a small leap for a giant..."

That wasn't right. "Leaping on the moon was..."

"No, no, no," said Mrs Scott crossly. "You'll have to learn to concentrate Fred. Stay behind at lunch-time."

Stay behind! But then he wouldn't be able to practise with Tom. Butterflies started to leap around Fred's stomach, rather like the astronauts on the moon.

"Never mind spaceman," said Tom trying to cheer him up as the lunch bell rang. "It's launch-time."

Fred sat gloomily at his table in the empty classroom, watching Mrs Scott marking books and listening to the ticking of the clock on the wall. Only two hours to the play.

"OK Fred. Off you go," she said finally, after what seemed like ages. "Try to stay down on earth for the rest of the day."

"And don't worry," she added in a much kinder voice. "You'll be fine this afternoon."

What did she mean, thought Fred, as he hurried off to lunch. He was going to forget his lines and be hopeless. Just like Alice Green said. He must find Tom!

Chapter Three

Tom had gone by the time Fred got to the lunch queue. There were only the dinner ladies chattering behind the counter.

"It's that Fred again," said the fat one, with a kindly wink at Fred. "Expect he's got his usual. Yes, chips, burger and chips."

Fred smiled weakly.

"No wonder you're so pale," said the other. "Now have some cabbage. That'll put colour in your cheeks." Fred shook his head. He didn't think he'd like green cheeks.

He went to find a seat in the crowded hall. But the only seat left was next to Alice.

"Such healthy food for a pirate chief," she said with a nasty smile as Fred sat down.

Fred sighed. Captain Hook wouldn't have these problems, he thought. Alice obviously didn't understand about food. She probably thought a barbecue was a line of people waiting for a haircut.

"And you'd better not eat all that," she went on. "Or you'll never fit into your costume this afternoon."

Fred pulled his two-headed alien face at Alice, quickly finished his burger, and hurried off to the playground to find Tom.

But he was too late again. Tom had gone to a dress rehearsal.

Fred groaned. Practising his lines was *much* more important than trying on clothes. He'd had his dress rehearsal the day before with the rest of the pirates, and they'd spent most of the time reading comics.

He wished he had his *Beano* with him now. He felt in his empty pockets and sighed. He would just have to practise his lines by himself.

"I'd give up if I were you," someone shouted in his direction. It was Alice Green again, playing football at the other side of the playground. "You'll be just as good at acting as you are at football. Useless!"

Fred felt angry. He was good at football. And as for Alice Green, her nose could run better than she could!

Fred picked up his script again. But now he was too cross to concentrate.

The idea of Alice Green as centre-back was ridiculous. More like a draw-back. Or better still, left-back. Left back in the classroom!

Frederick would show her, he thought to himself, his mind drifting off. Frederick would be a champion athlete ...

Frederick Fleetfoot, world famous footballer, swimmer, highjumper and hurdler, has just won another gold medal at the Olympic Games.

"It's amazing," says a voice on the loudspeaker. "Frederick is the fastest boy on earth. He has just run a two-minute mile!" *The crowd cheers and bells are rung ...*

Bells? Why bells? Suddenly Fred realised it was the school bell ringing. Already! He ran across the playground, arriving puffing and out of breath. And he *still* hadn't practised his lines.

Chapter Four

It was show time. The play was due to begin. The butterflies in Fred's stomach now felt like elephants on the rampage.

Teachers were hurrying around helping children with their costumes. Mrs Scott was blinking and flapping even more than usual.

And Fred could see Alice Green sitting in a corner, muttering her lines to herself.

"All right. Now you Fred," said Mrs Scott. "Try on this costume in the cupboard." Fred climbed into the large cupboard grinning, and started to put the costume on.

"Don't be so silly," said Mrs Scott as everyone began to laugh. "Put it on over there. Next to Tom."

But putting the costume on was easier said than done. That pile of chips had been a mistake, Fred thought, as he tried to fasten the jacket for the third time. It had fitted yesterday.

In the end, he had to breathe in while Tom quickly fastened all the silver buttons. He breathed out. A bit tight, but it would have to do.

"All ready," whispered Tom. "Good luck, Fred."

"Thanks, I'll need it," said Fred, peeping through the curtains at the audience. He could see his mum and dad in the third row. If he really were the Frederick of his daydreams, he wouldn't need luck. Frederick would make his mum and dad proud.

Mrs Scott drew the stage curtains to reveal Captain Hook's ship, *The Jolly Roger.* The audience clapped and then there was an excited hush as everyone waited for the show to begin.

Alice was the first to go on stage. Mrs Scott had to give her a little push, as she didn't seem to be able to move.

"I ... I ... I'm ..." Alice began, and went quiet.

"I'm Smee the pirate," whispered Mrs Scott from backstage.

Alice began again. "I ... I ... I'm ..." Alice had stage fright! She was nervous – and much worse than Fred was.

Alice stumbled through her speeches and had to be prompted at every line. The audience was beginning to fidget.

Then it was Fred's turn. He crossed and uncrossed his fingers, and walked on stage.

"Good afternoon," he said in what he hoped was his best pirate voice.

Then he bowed ... PING! A silver button shot off his jacket and bounced off the back of Mrs Scott's neck. She yelped.

"Um," Fred went on, glancing in Mrs Scott's direction, "I'm Captain Hook of *The Jammy Dodger*. I mean, Captain Hook of *The Dodgy Lodger*. No, *The Jolly Roger!*" Oh no! He was getting his words muddled up again.

He took a deep breath. PING! Another silver button flew off his jacket and landed in the audience. Fred pulled in his stomach.

"I'm looking for Peter Pan, who called me a codfish," he continued. "I'm going to light the fire!" That couldn't be right. "I mean, I'm going to fight the liar!"

Fred sighed ... PING! A third button shot off his jacket like a silver bullet and made the children in the first row jump.

Then Tom came on stage.

"Fight, Hook!" cried Tom as Peter Pan, and drew his sword.

"Fight Pan!" cried Fred as Captain Hook, and drew ... a rolled-up copy of the *Beano* from his sword holder. Fred gaped. He'd been wondering where that had got to!

Fred's cheeks were burning. This was terrible. He looked round for his mum and dad in the audience. His mum smiled and his dad gave him the thumbs up sign.

Fred took a big deep breath. Well, he thought, he might as well make the best of it. He stood up straight. He was *not* going to be hopeless, and the play was *not* going to be a disaster. And as for the *Beano* ... he'd make the best of that as well!

Fred looked at his mum and dad and grinned. "Defend yourself Pan!" he shouted, leaping towards Tom, waving the *Beano*. "This is your last hour!"

Tom smiled and raised his sword.

What followed was the best sword fight the school had ever seen. The audience clapped and cheered, and Mrs Scott laughed so much her glasses steamed up.

Fred began to enjoy himself. He found he could remember his lines after all, and he could make people laugh as well. The children all giggled when he made his buttons ping off. And everyone thought it was funny when he made his hook drop off, or caught it in the curtains when the crocodile was chasing him.

And when Alice forgot her lines, all Fred had to do was look menacing and wave his *Beano* at the audience, and everyone laughed (which gave Alice time to remember).

Fred was the star of the show. And he'd been ordinary old Fred, not Frederick.

At the end of the play, the applause went on for ages.

"You were really good Fred," Alice whispered as they bowed for the third time. "Better than I would have been, and I … I …" Fred thought she had stage fright again. "And I'm sorry I was mean to you."

Fred smiled. The frozen bean wasn't as bad as she looked.

The audience were shouting "bravo" and "encore" and other words Fred had heard on the telly.

The headteacher came on stage to congratulate them all.

"And a special thanks to you," she said. "Fred isn't it? Or should I call you Frederick?"

"No," said Fred, looking at the cheering audience and the proud faces of his mum and dad.

"Fred's just fine."